CONTAINER GARDENING OUTDOORS

by George Taloumis

PHOTOGRAPHS BY THE AUTHOR

SIMON AND SCHUSTER · NEW YORK

First printing

SBN 671–21141–2
Library of Congress Catalog Card Number: 76–189741
Designed by Eve Metz
Manufactured in the United States of America

A HELEN VAN PELT WILSON BOOK

CONTENTS

ACKNOWLEDGMENTS

FOR MAKING this book possible, I wish to thank the many amateur and professional gardeners in the parts of the world I have traveled for permitting me to photograph their container plants and gardens, the results of which grace these pages: Mr. and Mrs. Moses Alpers, Mr. and Mrs. George Berkey, Mrs. J. Brentlingen, Mrs. Eugene Cable, Mrs. H. A. Colby, Mrs. T. Jefferson Coolidge, Mr. and Mrs. Donald D. Dodge, Mr. Oliver Drackman, Mrs. Raymond Ellis, Daniel J. Foley, Mr. and Mrs. H. Crowell Freeman, Mrs. Calvin Hosmer, Mr. and Mrs. Nils R. Johaneson, Mrs. Frederick Kingsbury, Mrs. Austin Lamont, Mr. and Mrs. Paul Mellon, Mr. and Mrs. George S. Moore, Mrs. Louis Phaneuf, Mrs. Robert Ransohoff, Mrs. Deborah Risoldi, Mr. and Mrs. Gordon W. Roaf, Mr. and Mrs. Frank Ruggles, Mrs. Henry Strong, Mr. and Mrs. Charles Townsend, and Mrs. John G. Williams.

I am particularly grateful to Daniel J. Foley for lending me books in which to photograph drawings of historic container gardens, and to my editor, Helen Van Pelt Wilson, for her guidance and enthusiasm.

GEORGE TALOUMIS

Salem, Massachusetts
January, 1972

A variety of plants flourish in the author's sunny container garden. On steps and beside the gate: Otaheite orange, basil, rosemary, scented geraniums, parsley, chaenostoma, zonal geraniums, petunias, setcreasea, and variegated holly osmanthus.

1

PANORAMA
OF POSSIBILITIES

MOVABLE GARDENS have marvelous possibilities. They flourish everywhere, from Massachusetts to California and Hawaii, in Arizona, Texas, and Florida, and in Canada. They decorate townhouse gardens and balconies, country terraces and seaside cottages; they relieve the starkness of public buildings and city streets; they invite the hotel guest. Hanging from trees, suspended on walls, marshaled along steps, or clustered beside a gate, pots, boxes, tubs, planters, urns, kettles, strawberry jars, and other kinds of containers, filled with foliage and flowering plants, make easy-care outdoor decorations in shade and sun. Summering house plants and hobby collections of herbs or geraniums can be arranged outdoors as a container garden from May through October. The movable garden is indeed adaptable as no permanent, in-the-soil planting can ever be.

Enthusiasts who cannot garden in the open ground are discovering newfound pleasure in growing plants in many kinds of containers. Town houses are often designed with small, private patios, and condominiums have balconies where sun- or shade-loving plants may be grown. The apartment dweller, in city or town, can garden in window boxes or on a rooftop. Since we need green, growing things to offset the grimness of the concrete-and-steel structures that surround us, the container garden is the garden of the day—and of the future. And what better way to satisfy our need than with tubs of evergreens at a doorway, pots of geraniums along steps, or boxes with spring pansies and fall chrysanthemums on a tiny patio.

In New England, gardening in containers is very popular. Imitating the Old World, resort areas attract tourists with gay flower-filled boxes at windows, on porch railings, terraces, sundecks, and walls, and beside walks and driveways. Throughout the rest of the East Coast, large planters with honey locusts, maples, yews, junipers, and other trees and shrubs decorate sidewalks in downtown

Multihued coleus and trailing zebrinas with green-purple-silver leaves make a pleasing combination for the shady side of the house.

New York and Philadelphia. Small gardens in old cities, like Charleston and New Orleans, depend on pot plants for year-round color. In Florida, tubs with small palms and crotons serve as focal points on lawns, and planters at doorways are frequently filled with shrimp-plants, Chinese hibiscus, or orange-red ixoras.

Container gardening is widely practiced in California. Large circular or square planters, modular boxes, and redwood tubs of geometric design are, in fact, a California innovation. Many kinds of plants are grown in an equally wide assortment of containers—a fuchsia in a square box espaliered on a trellis, a kumquat in a low planter, a maidenhair fern in a ceramic bowl, a bird-of-paradise in an octagonal redwood tub, a tuberous begonia in a basket at the corner of a house. Trimmed pittosporums in Oriental jardinières, agapanthus in square metal planters, or sedums and succulents in flaring concrete dishes at the edge of a swimming pool are all part of the scene.

In dry Arizona, large clay pots, terra-cotta urns and bowls, and circular concrete containers, usually mulched with small stones, are common. Gardeners frequently select heat- and drought-tolerant succulents for exposed places, but are not reluctant to try gardenias, camellias, and such annuals as petunias, calendulas, dimorphothecas, and stock during the cooler winter months. On shaded verandas, you see many tropical plants—alocasias, bromeliads, dumb canes, dracaenas, and philodendrons.

Growing plants in containers is an easy way to garden. A hanging basket with a fuchsia can be suspended from a tree branch or the eaves of a house. A wall bracket for a pot of English ivy can be fastened to a fence or brick wall in a city garden. A window box with bright annuals is of interest inside as well as out. In fact, well-grown container plants bring beauty to any setting. They relieve monotonous stretches of pavement and soften harsh lines of terraces and retaining walls, steps, and stairways. The effect is strongly architectural, as a pair of urns with yews at an entrance. In the open ground, the same plants might easily pass unnoticed.

A weathered wooden barrel of strawberry plants stands beside a kitchen path that leads to an herb garden.

A GARDEN TO MOVE ABOUT

EXCEPT FOR very large boxes and planters, whether sta-
tionary or movable, containers can be readily shifted for a change
of scene. Like furniture in the house, they can be moved to achieve
a whole new effect. When plants have passed their peak, they can
be replaced by fresh stock. Some, as chrysanthemums, English daisies, spring bulbs, and pansies are always temporary, giving color
when needed, but removed from the stage when their performance
is over.

A well-grown container plant, foliage or flowering, can act as
a focal point in a garden border. It can be a feature at the end of a

*A topiary effect is achieved with metal epergnes topped with fig-
ures of children that are planted with strawberries. Pots of pink
geraniums and yellow lantanas are grouped around the entrance.*

White metal urns with pink geraniums and white petunias stand on each side of a millstone and accent a vista in a garden on the coast of Maine.

walk and, if large enough, a real point of interest. Spaces in flower borders, left by spring bulbs or perennials, such as bleeding-hearts, baby's-breath, or Oriental poppies, can be filled with pots of flowering annuals. If elevated on bricks, blocks of wood or interesting stones, they can be shown to better advantage. Since containers do not rest on the ground, they are hardly spattered by mud, and insects, like slugs and snails, are less apt to be troublesome. Many new homeowners are discovering that containers work well in areas around foundations where permanent plantings have not yet filled in.

[TOP, LEFT] *Red, pink, and white patience plants flourish in the shady entranceway of a house in a Philadelphia suburb.* [TOP, RIGHT] *Bare spaces in borders left by spring bulbs can be filled with container plants. Bricks steady the big pots of jade plant and geraniums.* [BELOW] *Geraniums in a concrete bowl and English ivies in clay pots summer in front of a garage that is used to store garden supplies.*

[TOP] *Moss-lined hanging baskets with pink tuberous begonias and mauve and rose fuchsias decorate a fence that gives privacy to a shady terrace on Nantucket Island.* [BOTTOM, LEFT] *Potted white geraniums along a broad flight of steps and great urns of the same plants placed on the walls dramatize this entrance.* [BOTTOM, RIGHT] *Pots of strawberries raised on inverted pots and set on a bench are decorative and easily cared for by elderly people who cannot stoop.*

You can start a container garden at almost any time of year; it depends on where you live. If you are busy in spring or move to a new home in midsummer, tubs of evergreens or annuals will give immediate effects. If you are away for the summer, pots of chrysanthemums set out on the terrace or by the doorway in the fall when you return will give bright splashes of color. Some city and suburban dwellers who summer within reasonable driving distance even bring their container plants back with them.

There is scarcely a limit to what you can grow. Indeed, the personality of the pot garden often revolves around unusual plants. Gardeners in cold areas of the country like to grow gardenias, bougainvilleas, Chinese hibiscus, lemons and oranges, and other tropicals in pots that are taken out in summer and brought indoors in winter.

Trees and shrubs present a more permanent form of container gardening and are especially valued for roof gardens and terraces. Trees give height and cast shade; shrubs form backgrounds for flowering plants. The number will depend on the size and design of the area but clutter should be avoided. An attractive terrace should

A shady terrace, restful on a hot day, is decorated with containers of fuchsia, patience plant, begonia, English ivy, and hosta. Swedish-ivy spills from hanging pots beside the doorway.

Redwood baskets of pink ivy geraniums flourish in the dappled light of a California lath house.

[LEFT] Handsome specimens of tuberous begonias in many colors are well displayed in a Carmel, California, patio.

[BELOW] A contemporary planter box in hot, sunny Athens is attractively filled with heat-tolerant and drought-resistant agaves, yuccas, cacti, and other succulents.

Graceful palms in Japanese soybean tubs line the driveway of a house on the Hawaiian island of Maui. Using a number of the same plants in the same kind of container is effective.

Containers with agaves, bananas, dracaenas, geraniums, and philodendrons remain outdoors in the warm-year-round climate of Tucson, Arizona.

have just enough interesting, well-grown plants of various kinds to make you want to linger there.

It is easy to coddle plants in containers. Each specimen can be watered according to its requirements for even moisture or slight dryness, and placed according to sun or shade preference. If house plants are taken outdoors for the summer, they can become an integral part of the pot garden. Keeping the container garden clean and attractive is a simple matter; dormant or diseased plants can be moved out of sight or discarded without leaving hard-to-fill gaps.

Containers can help solve problems of shade and wind. A difficult area under a large tree can be transformed into a terrace and decorated with baskets of ferns, spider plants (*Chlorophytum*), or Swedish ivies (*Plectranthus*) swinging from branches and pots of colorful coleus, fancy-leaved caladiums, or patience plants on the pavement. For the windswept seaside, where soil is light and sandy and huge outcroppings of rocks make gardening next to impossible, container plants offer a solution. If possible, select the leeward side of the house or erect a fence to cut the force of the wind, and include some trees and shrubs in large planters for height, enlivening them with transient flowering plants.

Where gardening by the open seashore is difficult because of wind and salt spray, sturdy geraniums and vinca flourish in summer in large boxes set on stone walls.

A handsome camellia in a redwood planter and potted orchids summer in a corner of a shady terrace.

FOR SMALL GARDENS

QUANTITIES OF POT PLANTS are well suited to small gardens where they give variety but occupy little space. If unusual kinds, like moonflower, stephanotis, or crossandra are included, the effect will be exotic. Tables, stands, and wall brackets can be used. If you have ever visited a tiny city garden or a courtyard in Spain or Italy, you recall how the wall surfaces are artistically adorned with numerous pot plants. Since gardens today are smaller, due to lack of help, the trend is toward up-and-down gardening. Instead of expanding horizontally, you can enlarge your gardening space vertically with pot plants fastened to walls and fences and hanging baskets suspended from eaves, posts, and trees. This imaginative form of gardening utilizes every bit of space—high or low walls, sides of houses, garages, or tool sheds—with boxes at windows.

Container gardening is ideal for busy people who have little time for plants, but still want a garden. It is the solution for those who are admittedly lazy, especially when it comes to the strenuous tasks of gardening in the ground. It also suits the elderly who can grow plants in containers placed on tables and stands, in raised boxes and planters, along steps, in easy-to-reach hanging baskets, and other places that do not require stooping and bending. If they are within reach, plants can be easily watered, fed, pruned, and sprayed. A work area, with a waist-high bench and cabinets for supplies, can make outdoor container gardening a pleasure for senior citizens.

FOR BALCONIES, ROOF GARDENS, AND MOBILE HOMES

WELL-DESIGNED BALCONY, rooftop, and sundeck gardens, where containers, large and small, make it possible to garden with-

Wind across a New York City penthouse garden has given this Russian-olive a picturesque form.

out soil, can be a delight outdoors. The attractive scenes they present can also be enjoyed from indoors, whether on the second, tenth, or fifteenth floor. In large cities, as Chicago or New York, gardens can be even higher. Whether placed on one side as a balcony or open all around as on a penthouse, the chief problem is wind. It is more severe at higher elevations, where it seems to blow even on "windless" days.

To make high-up gardening possible, erect barriers, fences, or screens with openings to admit some air. Bringing in soil is another problem; but it is worth the extra cost and effort to obtain good mixtures. To offset drying wind and provide shade for plants and people, set up umbrellas or build a lath or pergola section. Unless built-in drainage facilities are present, as they are in modern housing units, provide some means for water to flow away easily. *Be sure to erect guard rails and walls along edges for safety.*

To withstand wind, drying air, sun, and winter cold, some plants are better suited than others. This is especially true of trees and shrubs, which take more buffeting from wind. Since they cost more to buy, set up, and replace, they must be carefully selected. Evergreens that do well include Japanese cryptomeria, pitch, Scotch, white, and Japanese pines, and Norway, red, and white spruce. Yews are excellent, but arborvitae tend to windburn unless protected. Both gray and white birches, ginkgo, European linden, Moraine-locusts, Russian-olive, and pliable weeping willow are good performers. For flowering trees, choose Oriental cherries, crabapples, dogwoods, hawthorns, laburnums, and the mountain ash, which produces colorful fruit in fall.

Among shrubs, privets are the most adaptable, but others to consider are cotoneaster, euonymus, forsythia, shrub honeysuckle, lilac, pyracantha, flowering quince, and viburnum. Chinese fleece vine, sweet autumn clematis, woodbine, and wisteria are tolerant vines. Espalier plants that hug protecting walls thrive and are interesting and ornamental.

FOR MOBILE HOUSES

For the mobile or transient home a container garden, which itself is movable, is a decorative godsend. A window box with colorful dwarf dahlias, a strawberry jar with white sweet alyssum and blue lobelia, a hanging basket of yellow lantana or lush, green Swedish-ivy is most welcome. I have also seen delightful container gardens at mobile houses in the Southwest where the emphasis was on cacti and other succulents. Strategically placed boxes of plants conceal gas bottles and other utilities. Plants in containers can go far to transform the mobile unit, the old-time trailer, into a homey, inviting, and attractive place to live.

A hanging basket of ivy geranium and a box of zonal geraniums give a sense of home to this mobile house.

[BELOW] *The traditional blends with the contemporary as these modern containers filled with chrysanthemums stand beside the doorway of an old house in Marblehead, Massachusetts.*

2 🙰

IN OTHER TIMES
AND OTHER LANDS

THE HISTORY of pot gardening is fascinating. In the art of ancient cultures plants in containers are a common sight. Even nomad man is known to have carried with him, as he moved from place to place, containers of edible and medicinal plants.

The great cultures of Egypt, Assyria, Greece, and Rome practiced pot gardening to a high degree, with emphasis on ornamentals to adorn palaces, public buildings, and private houses of both rich and poor. At the same time—and earlier—the practice flourished in China, India, and other Oriental countries.

Due to climate, large-scale container gardening was essential around the Mediterranean and in the Near East, where summers are hot and dry and rainfall comes mostly during the winter months. Except for native vegetation—the deep-rooted trees and shrubs and the bulbs that bloom with the rains and then go dormant —plants are entirely dependent on artificial watering in summer. In containers, this was a simple procedure. Furthermore, the peoples of these civilizations apparently realized that a container could be ornamental, that form and texture could make it a thing of beauty in itself. With a well-grown plant, its aesthetic appeal increased.

Paintings of Egypt's Middle Period depict row upon row of pot plants. In ancient Greece, container plants were common features in courtyards where people dined outdoors and spent their leisure hours. The Romans observed the summer festival of Adonis by displaying flowering pot plants on rooftops, a practice also common to the Assyrians. Plant boxes were attached to the windows of Roman houses; Pliny, the Elder, referred to them as "mimic gardens" because they brought the country to the town. Fruit trees were set out in boxes on high towers in Pompeii, and the Emperor Justinian enjoyed a balcony garden that overlooked the sea.

In the Middle Ages, many exotic plants were set in colorful containers. In fifteenth-century Italy, trees and shrubs, including

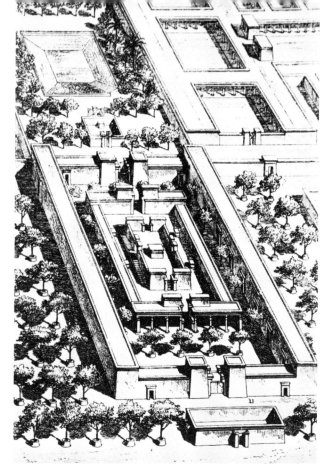

[ABOVE] *In a suggested restoration, a multitude of container plants decorate the fourteenth-century* B.C. *royal villa at Tell el 'Amârna in Egypt.* [BELOW] *A corner of a medieval garden features a central fountain and a bench of pot plants.*

Container plants are arranged in front of ornamental trellis work in a seventeenth-century French garden.

cypresses and oranges, were grown in huge containers. Villa gardens adopted the practice to the extent we see in Italy today, and container plantings became integral parts of gardens in France and England as the taste of the Italian Renaissance spread to those countries.

But pot gardening reached its peak in Spain, due to climate and also to the influence of the Moors, who came from the desert regions of northern Africa. The Moors, who thrilled to the abundance of water that came from the mountains in Spain, channeled it freely to pools and fountains. Portugal, also occupied by the Moors, was likewise influenced by the Moorish innovations.

In time, Austria, Switzerland, Germany, Scandinavia, and the Low Countries were similarly affected, each developing its own style of container gardening. In seventeenth-century Germany, urns and pots were scattered lavishly throughout formal gardens, and pots with flowering plants were set at windows. Large container plants, particularly oranges and lemons, stood out like sculpture in the palace and estate gardens of Holland, Belgium, Denmark, and Sweden.

IN EUROPE TODAY

ON A RECENT European trip, starting out at Shannon Airport, I saw window boxes and pots with geraniums and oxalis on the broad windowsills of thatched cottages throughout the Irish countryside. Wooden tubs with pink speciosum lilies graced walks at Birr Castle, where the thirty-foot tree-boxwoods are said to be the world's tallest. Bonsai chamaecyparis, oak, and larch accent the rectangular pool at Glengarriff, and ornate troughs with geraniums are outstanding at Powerscourt. Planters with annuals and dracaenas decorate the streets of Dublin and Cork as well as the cities and towns of England and Scotland.

Flowers in window boxes on London's department stores and banks change from spring tulips and azaleas to summer geraniums, followed by chrysanthemums and Jerusalem cherries. Tubs with blue-flowering agapanthus edge the pools at Hampton Court; tuberous begonias spill out of window boxes in Scotland, where gardening is a way of life. At Culzean Castle in Maybole, I recall dwarf dahlias set in ornate urns on the bright green turf.

Gardener carries a potted orange tree, from "Spring" by the Flemish painter, David Teniers the Younger, 1610–1690.

Sweet-bay standards in square tubs are an elegant note beside a London doorway.

In France, tubs with Japanese aucubas can be seen in front of Paris cafés. Huge planters at the Orangerie at Bagatelle Park in Paris hold oranges and lemons, as well as bird-of-paradise and agapanthus. The Orangerie at Villandry, the medieval fortress in the château country, is pure delight, with old tubbed orange trees set out along the terrace for their summer airing.

In Belgium and Holland, bulbs in low, contemporary planters bring spring color to sidewalks in front of theaters, museums, and other public buildings. In autumn, the planters are filled with heather. Magnificent in Holland is Kasteel Twickel at Delden, near the German border, with its 300-year-old tubbed orange trees and 150-year-old fuchsias. In these north European countries window boxes appear everywhere and pots are also set on broad window-sills. Huge, flaring concrete planters on the sidewalks of Bergen, Oslo, Stockholm, and Copenhagen glow with daffodils, azaleas, rhododendrons, marguerites, geraniums, and chrysanthemums.

Switzerland is brilliant with window boxes and chalet balconies are filled with pots of red and pink geraniums and trailing sprenger asparagus. Tuberous begonias grow luxuriantly there and also in the unspoiled, medieval Bavarian villages of Rothenburg

In the author's movable garden, browallia, fuchsia, geraniums, and lobelia bloom from summer through fall.

Ivy geraniums, begonias, and petunias cascade from hanging baskets and a window box at a restaurant.

A colorful, well-grown ivy geranium suspended near a doorway makes a garden by itself.

On a sunny deck overlooking a bay, boxes filled with dwarf dahlias and petunias are bright all summer long.

Cymbidium orchids moved outside a home greenhouse summer in the shade of a terrace tree.

Tubbed sweet bay plants lined up at the Orangerie of the Mirabell Palace Gardens in Salzburg, Austria.

Dwarf dahlias in a stone urn set on turf at Culzean Castle in Maybole on the west coast of Scotland.

Tuberous begonias bloom all summer if given early-morning or late-afternoon sunshine.

A wooden planter on wheels with cannas, coleus, and trailing white browallias.

Spring pansies flowering in a ceramic strawberry jar can be replaced later with sweet alyssum.

On the shaded terrace of the Nichols House Museum in Boston, pots of coleus and patience plants provide touches of color.

Virginia creeper, morning-glories, cannas, jasmines, podocarpus, and bougain-villeas flourish on a rooftop overlooking Constitution Square in Athens.

and Dinkelsbühl, not to mention cosmopolitan Vienna. Specimens of sweet bay, pruned to various forms, are grouped in front of the Orangerie at the Mirabell Palace Garden in Salzburg.

During five visits to Greece, I had opportunity to study gardens thoroughly. Even the most humble cottager performs miracles with plants in tin cans. Before my last trip, I vowed not to photograph any more tin-can gardens since I had enough slides for two lectures, but could not resist the one I came across in Corinth on a cloudy November afternoon, a colorful sight with huge elephant's-ears, pink geraniums, orange marigolds, multi-hued carnations, mauve Madagascar periwinkle, and large-leaved begonias.

Plants are also grown in handsome earthenware pots of simple, graceful design on terraces in the fashionable Athenian suburbs of Kifisiá, Psihikon, and Philothei, and in tiny, private courtyards of the Aegean islands—Aegina, Hydra, Póros, Míkonos, and Rhodes.

In Italy, container plants are seen now in shaded courtyards, on balconies and rooftops, and in such extensive villa gardens as Villa d'Este in Tivoli near Rome, where agaves in metal urns display their sculptured leaves; at Villa Lante in Viterbo, where lem-

In Athens the entrance to an apartment building is flanked with rubber plants and evergreen euonymus in glazed bowls.

ons grow in ornate terra-cotta pots; and at Borromeo Castle on Isola Bella in Lake Maggiore, where cascades of pink ivy geraniums and blue hydrangeas decorate balustrades. Balconies burst with bloom along the length of the Italian peninsula.

In Spain, small pots are attached to white-washed cottages and apartments, and large containers are scattered through public gardens, like Puerta Oscura in Málaga, where they are cemented on walls for protection against wind. Pools, the central feature of large and small gardens, are lined with pot plants, and in the Alhambra and Generalife in Granada, hundreds of clay pots are placed on walls. In Portugal, courtyards and balconies, even in the poor sections of old Lisbon, sparkle with decorated jardinières placed against blue-tiled walls. Ivy geraniums hang from the elaborately carved concrete urns at Queluz Palace, a popular attraction near Lisbon.

ORIENTAL BONSAI

THE ORIENTAL concept of growing plants in containers differs from the European in material and in culture. Greater emphasis is placed on bamboo, chamaecyparis, cryptomeria, holly, pieris, pine, and other evergreens, which are usually grown in porcelain bowls or hand-decorated vessels, and the plants are dwarfed. The art of bonsai originated in China, but later was adopted by the Japanese, who developed it to a higher degree. Except for these traditional bonsai, I was surprised to find so little pot gardening in Japan. Exquisite porcelain containers, primarily for evergreens, stand at dooryards of private homes, but the exuberance encountered in Europe is not found in the large Japanese gardens opened to the public. The exception is bonsai, which is much exhibited, the plants displayed on waist-high tables for easier viewing. But, following Western tradition, container plants appear around apartments and hotels and office buildings.

In Hawaii the same plants found in gardens are grown in containers. Philodendrons, scheffleras, Chinese hibiscus, ixoras, palms, dumb canes, gardenias, crotons, and bougainvilleas pruned into shrubs highlight terraces and sundecks. The Japanese soy tub is common, and moss-lined wire baskets with ferns, donkey-tail sedums, and orchids swing from eaves, lath roofs, and trees.

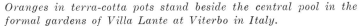

Oranges in terra-cotta pots stand beside the central pool in the formal gardens of Villa Lante at Viterbo in Italy.

3

CONTAINERS— THEIR INFINITE VARIETY

ANY RECEPTACLE in which a plant will grow can be used as a container. This includes glazed, unglazed, and plastic pots, tubs and buckets, window boxes and planters, hanging baskets, strawberry barrels, concrete urns and bowls, orange and lemon pots, metal urns, terra-cotta dishes, oil jars, and vessels made of fiber glass and various synthetics. Other possibilities are containers molded of zinc, tin, copper, or brass. Shiny aluminum is also fashioned into large modern planters, usually circular or square. All these are durable and non-breakable. On the West Coast, Japanese soy tubs are popular. Kettles, jugs and casks, crocks, nail kegs, and coal pails with plants can be seen along New England roads, and sometimes hollowed stones, rocks with crevices, and pieces of driftwood are used.

What constitutes the ideal container? First an attractive appearance, then durability, and it must be weatherproof. If kept outdoors in the north during the winter, it should not break when soil alternately freezes and thaws. In climates like the desert Southwest it must withstand very hot sun.

A container needs to be heavy enough to stand up against average wind. Ceramic pots, tubs, boxes, and planters are usually strong enough but lightweight plastic pots are not. If containers like metal urns are valuable, secure them with concrete at the base or chain them to railings to prevent vandalism. Avoid containers smaller than six inches. Plants in them give a spotty effect, for they are not in scale outdoors where a garden has the vast sky for a ceiling. Furthermore, they dry out quickly in hot weather, requiring watering two or three times a day, and they fall over when it's windy.

Clay pots have been around a long time. The unglazed types are inexpensive and durable with a natural texture that makes them appear at home in the garden. Though the color of new pots is

[ABOVE, LEFT] *Petunia 'Sugar Plum' in a strawberry jar needs regular pruning so that the form and surface of the jar are not entirely concealed.* [ABOVE, RIGHT] *A low concrete bowl holds spring pansies to be followed by dwarf orange and yellow marigolds in summer.* [BOTTOM, LEFT] *A synthetic container, on an Arizona terrace, is one of the many new kinds available to gardeners.* [BOTTOM, RIGHT] *A spectacular potted cut-leaved philodendron is placed in a decorative plastic bowl on a stand to set off the plant and reduce transpiration through the walls of the clay pot.*

[ABOVE] *This Japanese soy tub, a container much used in Hawaii and on the West Coast but available elsewhere, holds a budding camellia.*

[LEFT] *A tall podocarpus is set off by a decorated Japanese ceramic bowl beside a doorway in California.*

harsh, it soon mellows. However, with time fertilizer salts and moss collect on the outside. This is unsightly, though hardly noticeable in old gardens.

Because clay pots are porous, soil dries out quickly. On the other hand, roots breathe easily and there is less rotting than in plastic pots. If the pot soil is mulched with peatmoss, wood chips, pebbles, or crushed stones, it will stay moist longer. In any event, unglazed pots—traditional or contemporary—are an excellent choice.

GLAZED CONTAINERS

GLAZED TERRA-COTTA containers enliven a scene. Solid colors are best, since they complement rather than detract from plants. The handsome decorated types are better suited to foliage than to flowering plants. Because of the glaze, they dry out more slowly and fertilizer salts and moss do not collect.

Plastic pots are widely used today. Lightweight and non-breakable, they hold moisture longer than clay, at least twice as long, and they are easy to clean with a brush or cloth dipped in hot, soapy water. Mottled plastic pots are distracting, but solid white, gray, and soft green pots harmonize with all plants. Where wind is a problem, plastic pots can be inserted in clay pots, tubs, or boxes, the space between filled with soil or peatmoss to give more weight.

When plants are suspended in baskets at eye-level, they have an air of distinction. The old-time basket, a rounded wire form lined with moss, is now recommended only for quite large plants. In common use for plants of average size are white or gray plastic bowls and standard clay and plastic pots that are suspended with strong wire clamps. Redwood baskets—square, triangular, rectangular, or conical—are very popular.

A barrel makes a fine container. Cut down a tall one, and if hoops slip, secure them with small nails. Bore holes in the bottom for drainage, and treat the wood with a nontoxic wood preservative, like Cuprinol. Rarely do we see the old-fashioned wooden strawberry barrel, but the modern ceramic counterpart has pockets at the sides for dwarf ivies, houseleeks, lobelias, petunias, and sweet alyssum.

[BELOW, LEFT] *A low concrete container, sturdy and weatherproof, holds an accent plant of the scented geranium 'Prince Rupert.'* [BELOW, RIGHT] *Large contemporary vessels, each different in design, provide ample root space for shrubs like Japanese pieris and rhododendron.*

[ABOVE, LEFT] *A moss-lined wire basket contains sufficient soil for a trailing purple lantana that requires watering twice a day in hot weather.* [ABOVE, RIGHT] *In a Maine garden an antique butter churn mellowed by time is suited to the homey charm of soft pink geraniums.* [BOTTOM, LEFT] *An old-fashioned black kettle on a tripod makes an appropriate container for red geraniums in a country setting.* [BOTTOM, RIGHT] *An octagonal tub, weathered to soft brown, features a large bird-of-paradise plant on a patio.*

[ABOVE, RIGHT] *A hollowed-out log serves as container for colorful petunias at a summer home on Mt. Desert Island, Maine.* [ABOVE, LEFT] *A nicely designed window shelf holds a number of pots of pink geraniums.* [BOTTOM, RIGHT] *A shelf with openings to support pots at rim level is a variation on the conventional window box and here holds a tuberous begonia and a patience plant.* [BOTTOM, LEFT] *Kalanchoes and other succulents are often planted in hollow driveway posts in California.*

4 ⚡

MULTITUDE OF PLANTS FOR MOVABLE GARDENS

EVERY GARDEN offers opportunities for the effective placement of containers. A graceful fuchsia beside a doorway, a row of red geraniums on a long flight of steps, dwarf orange and yellow marigolds at the base of a patio wall make dramatic accents that are easily achieved. You can group pots of sun-loving yellow and white marguerites at the corner of house or garage or set a specimen agapanthus, camellia, or fishtail palm for interest on a lawn. Container plants can interrupt a long stretch of wall or fence, disguise unsightly structures, screen undesirable views, add color along the top of a retaining wall, or decorate a swimming pool.

ON THE TERRACE

THE TERRACE is an excellent place to enjoy a handsome specimen of fragrant jasmine, ginger, or citrus, or you can group plants where the beauty of each can be appreciated at close range. Attach a pot plant to a lamppost or a small planter to a roadside mailbox. Mass shade-loving hydrangeas or patience plants under a big tree, place a tub of annuals on top of a tree stump, soften walls with a tracery of morning-glories, clematis, or climbing nasturtiums.

If you are gardening on a rooftop, you could grow a crabapple or a dogwood in a large planter for flowers, shade, and fruit. In the North you might prefer a silverbell, styrax, or franklinia; in the South, an orange tree. Certain unusual trees and shrubs can be grown in containers—fig, Japanese plum, pomegranate, or the contorted willow (*Salix matsundana tortuosa*). The scale of plants is always to be considered. Tall cosmos and African marigolds are not

[RIGHT] *With patience and skill many plants can be trained as bonsai. This exquisite pine was exhibited at Expo '70 in Osaka, Japan.*

[ABOVE, LEFT] *White, biennial canterbury bells in a white tub decorate a terrace at night.* [ABOVE, RIGHT] *Evergreens like Japanese privet can be trained into delightful topiary forms.*

[LEFT] *The tender shrub, hebe, is noted for its spikes of blue flowers that appear all summer.*

Thrinax palm is a handsome house plant that can be taken to the terrace for the summer.

[BELOW, LEFT] *On the patio the white-flowering star-of-Bethlehem* (Campanula iso-phylla) *shines in the sun and is luminous.*

[ABOVE] *Pots of gray-leaved dusty mil-ler command attention at the top of the garden steps.*

A specimen of cordyline at a doorway in Yokohama, Japan, demonstrated Japanese interest in foliage rather than flowering plants, and on ornamental containers.

[BELOW] *Pungent rosemary, hardy in frost-free areas, can be trained to tree form.*

[ABOVE] *Succulent crassulas are common pot plants in California gardens and many produce showy flowers.*

for window boxes, and wax begonias in three-foot-deep planters are lost. Otherwise, you can grow lilies in pots on your terrace or cannas in boxes along the driveway. You can enjoy rhododendrons in planters, hostas and daylilies in large pots, hybrid tea roses in tubs, and cherry tomatoes in hanging baskets.

IN THE EVENING

MAKE PLANS for container plants that are attractive at night. For working people, evenings and weekends are times when their gardens can be enjoyed. Simple, yet effective lighting makes a night garden possible—a lantern or two attached to the side of the house or a post, spotlights on a doorway with a grouping of pot plants, a picturesque specimen tree with hanging baskets, or a pool with boxes of colorful annuals. Suspend Japanese paper lanterns overhead for a romantic effect, and dine to the soft glow of candlelight. Good lighting is worth some effort and expense, as it blends day with night and extends the hours of the garden's or terrace's usefulness.

With or without lights, the container garden becomes enchanting at night with white flowering plants, particularly if they are fragrant. White is a "color" that shows up in the dark. Even without a moon, white geraniums, lilies, petunias, roses, and tuberous begonias stand out. Two good scented plants are flowering tobacco and moonflower, which open at night. The little-known moonflower is an annual vine that can be trained on wall or trellis. Its large blossoms, to five inches across, open at dusk and close in the morning. Give seed an early start indoors for plants to grow in large pots or tubs in a warm, sunny location. Angel's-trumpet (*Datura*) is another outstanding white-flowering annual with large blooms that are sweet-scented.

Fragrance in the pot garden can also be introduced with carnation, frangipani, gardenia, heliotrope, jasmine, lemon, lily, mignonette, orange, pansy, petunia, pittosporum, rose, stock, sweet alyssum, sweet pea, and tuberose. For daytime pleasure, select scented geraniums, whose fragrant oils are released in hot sun—fingerbowl, lemon, peppermint, or rose. Include herbs for fragrance and cooking—basil, costmary, lavender, lemon verbena, rosemary, sage, thyme, and winter savory.

Pots of hybrid lily bulbs bring fragrance to the terrace on summer evenings.

[RIGHT] *The variegated evergreen Japanese euonymus and pittosporum thrive in hot, sunny exposures.*

[LEFT] *Dwarf 'Bonanza' peaches are attractive with or without fruit when grown in containers.*

5 ❧

HANGING PLANTS
IN LEAF AND FLOWER

EVERY HOUSE and garden offer opportunities to display hanging baskets attractively. A doorway, a lamppost, a porch, a fence, a pergola, a lathhouse, or a tree branch all present appropriate locations. In addition to the common moss-lined wire baskets, a number of more interesting hanging containers are available, as those of redwood in square, triangular, rectangular, and octagonal shapes and the circular plastic containers, in white, gray, or green. Clay containers in various shapes are equipped with chains and saucers to catch water, and standard plastic pots become hanging baskets when strong wire clamps are attached to them. Unusual copper, brass, and zinc containers can also be found, and many strong woven baskets that are suspended by wires or rope.

For large specimens of lantana, fuchsia, or ivy geranium the wire baskets are still recommended. The advantage of plastic pots and baskets is that they are lightweight and hold moisture longer than clay, which dries out fairly fast. Select in any case, the type of container that is best suited to the location, but avoid any less than six inches in diameter, as these dry out too quickly in hot weather.

Secure hanging baskets, particularly large ones, safely with strong hooks, wire, chain, or rope to prevent disasters in wind. Except for plants in sheltered places—a lath house or secluded terrace corner—take them down in a violent storm.

BUY GROWN PLANTS

THE QUICKEST WAY to have an attractive hanging basket plant is to buy a well-grown specimen in spring. Since it is already growing in a good soil mixture, it will not require repotting, unless you want it to attain large size. Keep it well watered through summer, and feed it every two to three weeks to support new growth

[RIGHT] *Fuchsia 'Mme. Cornelissen' in a clay pot with saucer attached swings from the branch of a specimen crabapple.*

[LEFT] *A fuchsia in a moss-lined wire basket, hung from the eaves of a house near the sea, dries out quickly in hot weather.*

In warm areas free from frost, decorative wire baskets of ferns, as these in Hawaii, stay out all year.

The white form of star-of-Bethlehem (Campanula isophylla) *is a showy trailer for hanging baskets. It is hardy in California.*

Lath protects delicate blooms of tuberous begonias from wind and sun.

[OPPOSITE] Begonia richmondensis *grows luxuriantly in a moss-lined wire basket that allows plenty of root run.*

and encourage flowering. If you prefer to grow your own basket plants, start with seedlings of pansies or petunias or small fuchsias or lantanas. This method is less expensive, and you can enjoy watching the plants develop. With facilities, you can start several new baskets at interims, particularly annuals, as drummond phlox, lobelias, nemesias, and petunias, which reach maturity in six to eight weeks.

Plants need not all be flowering types. Foliage plants are also handsome, especially variegated kinds, as English ivy, golden archangel (*Lamium*), spider plant (*Chlorophytum*), and zebrina. As a group, they flourish without sun, and answer the question of what to grow in the shade of trees or buildings. If you want flowers (in shade), select achimenes, episcia, patience plant, and thunbergia.

WATER REGULARLY

PLANTS in hanging baskets thrive in the same soil and with the same care as plants in other containers, but they require more water. Exposed to sun and wind, they dry out faster. Avoid letting them go limp, since some, as browallia or fuchsia, may not recover fully. If containers are within easy reach, watering is no problem, but for overhead plants, you need a ladder or stool or even a pulley system to water, feed, prune, and remove faded blooms and any yellow leaves.

Bring hanging baskets indoors in winter unless you want them for outdoor decoration. They deteriorate in cold weather, and freezing soil cracks clay and plastic. For winter decoration, remove soil from containers and insert crumpled chicken wire, tied across the top to hold greens and berried branches.

6☙

CONTAINERS
IN FOUR SEASONS

WE WHO LIVE in cold climates plan our gardens for the four seasons. The container garden, being adaptable, can be readily changed from season to season, even from week to week. Emphasis can be given one season, as spring when the garden is at its loveliest, or summer when you move to a cottage by the sea or in the mountains. Spring comes strongest in cold climates, yet its presence is also felt in frost-free areas. No matter where you live, you can make a dramatic start with pansies and pans of crocus, followed by daffodils, hyacinths, and tulips. Introduce the refreshing blue of forget-me-nots, a cool note with warm red, orange, and yellow flowers. Tender azaleas, blue phlox, calceolarias, cinerarias, Easter lilies, English daisies, hydrangeas, primroses, violas, and scented wallflowers are other spring flowers to plant in containers.

For summer, select free-flowering annuals—calendulas, marigolds, and snapdragons—but have some perennials, too—daylily, gloriosa daisy, liatris, lythrum, and phlox. Make room for the tender summer bulbs—calla-lilies, dahlias, gladiolus, montbretias, tigridias, tuberoses, and tuberous begonias. Not only strawberries, but houseleeks, lobelias, dwarf petunias, and sweet alyssum can be grown in strawberry jars. Cannas and castor-oil plants are dramatic and for sun-baked areas, California poppies, mesembryanthemums, Madagascar periwinkles, portulacas, and venidiums are good choices.

Dried strawflowers that close when wet and reopen when dry are among the best flowers to use with greens in a winter window box.

Give thought to containers in autumn, a season we often overlook. If you go away for the summer, you may prefer an autumn pot garden to a spring or summer one. Fall is usually a pleasant season, with sunny, mellow days that beckon us outdoors. If severe frost threatens, small containers can be taken inside to basement, breezeway, or entrance hall for the night, and brought outdoors again in the morning.

TREES AND SHRUBS

CONSIDER trees, shrubs, and vines with colorful foliage—amelanchier, Boston ivy, flowering dogwood, enkianthus, dwarf winged euonymus, tatarian maple, sassafras, sourwood, and Virginia creeper. Include some fruiting plants—mountain-ash, bittersweet, cotoneaster, crabapple, firethorn, holly, nandina, and viburnum. Some plants are late bloomers—Chinese fleece-vine, common witch-hazel, franklinia, Japanese bush clover, rose of Sharon, and sweet autumn clematis.

[BELOW, LEFT] *Bulbs of the fall-flowering lavender* Crocus speciosus *planted in this ceramic pot on September 23 were in full bloom when photographed on October ninth.* [BELOW, RIGHT] *Plants of flowering kale potted from the garden stay decorative until a killing frost.*

White tubs of greens with bittersweet and bayberry adorn an autumn terrace.

Chrysanthemums bring gaiety to the autumn picture. It is hardly possible to have too many at doorways, on steps, on terraces. The little-known flowering kale, an ornamental vegetable with crinkly mauve and green leaves, is at its best in cool weather. Buy florist plants or raise this from seed. It's as easy as cabbage, and mature plants can be potted from the garden in September. There are also the late-flowering perennials—heleniums, Japanese anemones, the lavender mistflower (*Eupatorium coelestinum*), and the deep-blue leadwort (*Ceratostigma plumbaginoides*), a good ground cover under trees in planters.

As a group, annuals bloom well into fall, but some are more resistant than others to cold weather and light frosts—calendulas, marigolds, nicotianas, salvias, snapdragons, and sweet alyssum. Geraniums, usually treated as annuals, are also undaunted by cold. Ageratum, balsam, coleus, patience plant, and zinnia are too tender to make a late fall show.

Dwarf dahlias can be grown in individual pots or window

boxes. Cannas put on a good show but succumb to early frosts. Autumn crocus and colchicum bring a touch of spring to the autumn scene, and wild cyclamen and sternbergias also bloom in fall.

Evergreens are backbone plants for the container garden. Given good care, they flourish for years. Gray-green junipers tolerate drying winds and hot sun. The compact, slow-growing dwarf Alberta spruce (*Picea glauca albertina*) takes up little space on the small patio. Dependable broad-leaved evergreens include barberries, cherry-laurel, hollies, Japanese pieris, leucothoe, and rhododendrons for the North; aralias, bamboos, Southern magnolia, camellias, Chinese hollies, and nandina for the South.

WINTER DECORATIONS

NOVEMBER AND DECEMBER are the months to decorate containers for winter. By that time, plants have been killed by frost, although soil has not frozen. Empty window boxes are a forlorn sight but filled with greens and berries, they look gay, particularly if they are painted a bright color.

One of the best greens for window boxes is balsam fir, which does not shed. Red, white and pitch pines and Douglas fir are others. Branches can also be pruned from the garden yews. Other useful winter evergreens are euonymus, hollies, junipers, leucothoe, pieris, and rhododendrons. Avoid hemlocks and spruces because their needles drop.

The easiest way to use cut evergreens is to insert them in soil. If all soil has been removed from the window boxes, crumpled chicken wire with a section nailed across the top will hold branches in position. Greens alone can be used but berries add color—orange bittersweet, pink California pepper berries, gray bayberry, and red-black alder. Red-dyed ruscus, an evergreen plant with prickly leaves, lasts all winter. Dried strawflowers—gold, orange, red, and pink—can also be used. The flowers close when wet, but open when dry. Cones, natural or slivered or gilded, can be wired among the greens.

Various other dried plant material holds up outdoors in winter: orange Chinese lanterns; the fruits of crabapples, hawthorns, and viburnums; gourds and artichokes; seed pods of clethra, iris,

Balsam fir and the berries of bittersweet and bayberry make a pleasing combination for a winter window box.

Japanese tree-lilac, magnolia, milkweed, silverbell, and teasel. The dried blooms of tansy and hybrid yarrows supply gold accents.

7

FOR TOWN AND SHOP AND PARK

AMERICANS traveling in Europe are impressed by the window boxes that decorate public buildings and apartments in London, Paris, Madrid, Lisbon, Vienna, Rome, and Athens, and in small towns as well. They admire the container plants they see in courtyards and patios, particularly in the hot, dry Mediterranean countries. When they return, they are often impelled to work for the beautification of their own city or town, for increasing industrialization has emphasized our need for green things growing around our buildings of concrete and steel.

Visitors to other countries are discovering similar beautification programs with container plants. In Japan, I saw scarlet azaleas in rectangular planters on the ramps of the new Akasaka Hotel in Tokyo, and wooden planters and boxes of pansies of English daisies along the streets of Osaka, the city of the 1970 Exposition. A small photography shop in Kyoto attracted attention with boxes at different levels filled with calendulas, pansies, and pinks.

In Honolulu, I saw built-in planters of fragrant frangipani set above the garage entrance of an apartment building and large pots of acalyphas, ixoras, philodendrons, and scheffleras in front of hotels and motels. Flaring planters of flamboyant bougainvilleas were arranged around swimming pools, and ferns in baskets swayed from the broad eaves of restaurants.

IN NEW ENGLAND

IN THIS COUNTRY, Mrs. Lyndon B. Johnson helped spark the city beautification program, but even before that Boston, Chi-

[OPPOSITE] *Evergreen topiaries in different containers stand at the corner of a men's shop in Tucson, Arizona.*

Purple lantanas on parking meters above the reach of trucks and vandals are an innovation in Rockport, Massachusetts.

Maples in large concrete planters are a familiar sight on streets in downtown Portland, Oregon.

[ABOVE] *Fuchsias adorn east-facing window boxes at the home office of* Down East *magazine in Camden, Maine.* [BELOW] *Window boxes at the post office in Nobleboro, Maine, are a part of the town's beautification program.*

cago, New Orleans, New York, Philadelphia, Phoenix, Portland, San Francisco, and Seattle had demonstrated that yews, Kwanzan cherries, and Japanese privets in concrete containers along sidewalks improved the looks of a metropolis and that window boxes of azaleas, chrysanthemums, marigolds, pansies, and tulips attracted business. Suspended from lampposts, baskets of ivy geraniums, lobelias, sweet alyssum and vinca relieved the starkness of city streets.

In Boston, twenty-seven rectangular and twenty-five circular permanent brick planters along Tremont Street present a color parade from spring bulbs to fall chrysanthemums. Historic Beacon Hill in the center of the city is decked, summer and winter, with window boxes that enhance the charm of town houses of architectural excellence. An annual contest sponsored by the Beacon Hill Garden Club maintains enthusiasm for these decorations. The fishing port of Gloucester, Massachusetts, installed large planters on islands in the center of roads and at intersections, a most successful project. Nearby Rockport has already earned a nationwide reputation for its containers of fuchsias, lantanas, and pink ivy geraniums that are attached to parking meters above the easy reach of vandals.

In Essex, Massachusetts, the Village Restaurant is decked with baskets of lush pink ivy geraniums and rose-flowering *Begonia richmondensis*, more than three feet long. In Concord, the town of Emerson, Thoreau, and Alcott, a container beautification program was recently started with tubs on sidewalks and at street intersections that featured gold and rust chrysanthemums in the fall. For decades, Camden, Maine, has been noted for its lamppost baskets, and there are window boxes at the small post office in Nobleboro. Newport, New Hampshire, had the original idea of clamping metal containers of petunias to parking meters in the center of broad Main Street, where a high school boy sees to the watering. Lynn, Massachusetts, placed large wooden boxes of arborvitae along downtown streets. They were attractive winter and summer but died after a few seasons due to lack of water. Wherever container plants are used, plans must be made for regular care.

Unique is Constitution Plaza, a nine-acre complex of business buildings in Hartford, Connecticut. The maintenance of the roof garden has been of high quality so that the effect is always good. Above a multiple-level garage are large planters of little-leaf lin-

Clipped evergreen Japanese privets surround Union Square in the heart of San Francisco.

Aluminum boxes attached to lampposts in Beverly, Massachusetts, are always decorated for Christmas.

dens, Moraine-locusts, and weeping willows, and smaller ones with specimen magnolias and weeping cherries. Below, around the complex, are concrete planters with sugar maples underplanted with pansies in spring.

In Penn Center Mall surrounding City Hall in Philadelphia, planters with crabapples, Kwanzan cherries, Moraine-locusts, Osage oranges, and styraxes give height, beauty of blossom and foliage, and striking winter form. Smaller planters hold yews; others, daffodils and tulips in spring, then summer annuals. Also in Philadelphia is the nationally known Neighborhood Garden Association program of Mr. and Mrs. James Bush-Brown aimed at beautifying blighted areas with window boxes. Started in 1953, it has served as a model for programs in other cities.

[OPPOSITE] *Concrete planters with wild orange trees* (Prunus caroliniana) *enhance a shopping arcade in downtown Phoenix.*

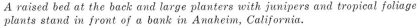

A raised bed at the back and large planters with junipers and tropical foliage plants stand in front of a bank in Anaheim, California.

A heavy stone trough at the Demonstration Garden in Golden Gate Park, San Francisco, is planted with drought-tolerant echeverias and other succulents.

A bottomless planter with palms and containers of philodendrons and ficus make shopping at Biltmore Fashion Park in Scottsdale, Arizona, a pleasant pastime.

[ABOVE] *In November, yellow chrysanthemums and English ivies enliven Paley Park at East Fifty-third Street near Fifth Avenue in New York City. Yews replace chrysanthemums in winter.* [BELOW] *Japanese privets, azaleas, and ivy in contemporary planters are a contrast to other plantings at colonial Williamsburg, Virginia.*

FLORIDA AND THE WEST COAST

IN FLORIDA, tastefully landscaped banks and business blocks emphasize containers with allamandas, caladiums, crotons, ixoras, and shrimp-plants. In Tucson, Arizona, sidewalks display large planters with Japanese privets and Joshua trees. Palms and southern cherry-laurel (*Prunus caroliniana*) grace sidewalks in Phoenix. In winter, planters at the Maricopa County Governmental Complex are radiant with orange and yellow calendulas. The Biltmore Fashion Park in Scottsdale is a garden of planters and movable contemporary containers with dracaenas, ficus, palms, philodendrons, pittosporums, and trailing sprenger asparagus.

Large container-grown trees and shrubs are a common sight along sidewalks in California—acacias, firethorns, oleanders, olives, podocarpus, Southern magnolias, and sweet bay. Camphor trees are featured in Fresno, Italian cypresses in Los Gatos, palms in the bottomless containers in Santa Barbara, and Japanese privets in San José and around Union Square in San Francisco. Palms, fuchsias, lantanas, and wax begonias thrive in the roof garden of the Fairmont Hotel in San Francisco and at Kaiser Center in Oakland, where the green sward is set off by olive trees and planters with petunias and drummond phlox.

In the summer-dry climate of the Golden State, containers are useful because they are easily watered. You see junipers and screw pines (*Pandanus*) in front of banks, tubs of oranges and kumquats at open-air restaurants, and window boxes with dwarf tuberous begonias at shops. Maples in contemporary planters line the streets of downtown Portland and Seattle. In Victoria, British Columbia, moss-lined wire baskets on lampposts are cascades of geraniums, lobelias, Mexican marigolds, nasturtiums, petunias, schizanthus, and viscarias.

Containers also appear at motels, churches, fire stations, airports, and particularly filling stations, the last place they would be expected. Tires and batteries mingling with boxes of petunias and other annuals are an everyday sight. Operators of filling stations who tend the plants certainly deserve praise. Today permanent planters are often built into apartment houses, offices, and industrial plants. Some planters are bottomless and set along foundations, others are free-standing, as in paved areas.

Plastic containers with petunias are fastened to parking meters along Main Street in Newport, New Hampshire. They are watered by a school boy in summer.

Boxes with gay petunias hobnob with tires and cans of oil at a filling station.

Boxes with pink geraniums and white petunias beautify the front of a small New England chapel.

Growing plants under city conditions presents certain problems—polluted air, soot and grime, strong drafts of wind among tall buildings, shade from buildings and large trees, heat from pavements, light reflected from large plate-glass areas, and excessive summer and winter temperatures. Yet plants grow well in cities if they get good care. This involves some effort—watering twice a day in hot weather, hosing foliage frequently to remove grime, bracing trees and shrubs to avoid breakage by wind and snow, spraying to control pests.

If soil is fertilized at planting time and plants are watered regularly, they will usually flourish. In town projects, schoolboys may be induced to water plants through summer; shop-owners are almost always willing to water containers on sidewalks. Firemen can be commissioned to water high hanging baskets in early morning hours when traffic is quiet, a plan that has worked well in Victoria, British Columbia.

Maintenance depends on a permanent crew. Without water, small plants shrivel and may die in just one long hot weekend. For success with container plants in cities, select tough, hardy, drought-resistant trees and shrubs, prune to reduce leafage, maintain mulches, and where possible install an automatic watering system.

There is such a thing as easy maintenance, but no such thing as no maintenance. More than a century ago, Henry David Thoreau, speaking for a rural America, had civic beautification in mind when he wrote: "It would be worth the while if in each town there were a committee appointed to see that the beauty of the town received no detriment." Sound advice we can adopt today from coast to coast.

[ABOVE] *Little-leaf lindens in planters, with pachysandra as ground cover, grow at Constitution Plaza in Hartford, Connecticut, in a garden above a garage.* [BELOW] *Square planters with yews, geraniums, and Baltic ivy stand in a pool at Constitution Plaza in Hartford, Connecticut.*

8 ✠

PLANTING
AND CARE

To a great extent, the success of a container garden depends on soil. Given a proper mixture with sufficient humus, fertilizer, and moisture, plants grow well, even under adverse conditions. In containers, soil requirements are more easily met than in open ground. The all-purpose mixture is recommended for most plants, and is the one to try if in doubt. It consists of two parts garden soil, one part sand or perlite, and one part peat moss, leafmold, or other humus, with a sprinkling of superphosphate and a complete fertilizer or the amount recommended on the package. Ingredients are combined with the soil in a just-moist condition. I use this mixture for all my plants, adding a little extra sand or perlite to assure good drainage for those that need it.

Before potting, clean most containers with a damp cloth or sponge, but scrub pots if salts or scum are in evidence. Use a stiff brush and hot, soapy water. Give tubs and wooden boxes a fresh coat of paint, two if they need it. As you select containers, keep in mind the ultimate size of the plants. Containers for tall trees and shrubs should be one-third their height. One plant for each container is usually right, but several can be grouped in a low container, for instance, three lantanas in a tub. Space annuals and other small plants a few inches apart for immediate effect. Even set so close, they will flourish in well-prepared soil with a good feeding program. In a four-foot box, allow six geraniums, five cascade petunias, and five or six trailers such as vinca or English or Swedish-ivies.

POTTING PROCEDURE

If you have potted house plants, you know the technique. First place drainage material in the bottom of the container. One

To facilitate drainage in window boxes, place large pieces of crock, round side up, over holes before adding soil. A lining of copper or zinc makes boxes last longer.

large piece of crock (broken flowerpot), rounded side up, is enough for a four- to six-inch pot. Above it spread one to two inches more of crocking or pebbles or gravel. Larger containers, ten inches or more across, require bigger pieces and a deeper drainage layer— up to three or four inches. A piece of burlap or a thin layer of sphagnum moss placed above the drainage layer helps to prevent clogging of openings. For containers without drainage holes, as a jardinière or strawberry jar, use a layer of drainage material one-third the depth to catch excess water and keep it from settling around the roots.

Spread a layer of soil mixture, depth depending on size of container and size of root-ball, over the drainage material. Add more soil, enough so the root-ball rests half an inch to an inch below the rim of the containers—deeper for trees and shrubs. (This space is left at the top to receive water.)

Fill in with more soil, firming it with your fingers or a potting stick. Press the soil down gently to eliminate air pockets, but avoid so much pressure that fine roots are injured. Finally, water well;

several applications may be needed if the soil is somewhat dry. Set plants in the shade for a few days so that they can recover from the shock of transplanting more readily than in sun.

TREES AND SHRUBS

To PREPARE window boxes for small plants, fill with soil almost to the top. Then, with a trowel or fingers, make holes large enough to accommodate the ball of soil of each specimen. Set the plants in place and fill in with soil, firming it around the base of each one. Be sure to leave enough space at the top of the box for water.

Planting trees and shrubs is not always a one-man task. You may need a helper. When plants do not readily slip out of old containers, you may have to tear or break these apart while holding up the plants to keep roots intact; use tin cutters to cut tin. Though you may have to pull and tug plants to remove them, be gentle so as to prevent the ball of soil from breaking apart, thus damaging roots.

After potting and watering, apply a mulch, an invaluable aid to container plants. Whether you use an organic mulch—peatmoss, shredded bark, or wood chips, or an inorganic material—stones, pebbles, or plastic, its purpose is to hold moisture, check weed growth, keep soil cool with less hot-and-cold fluctuation, and improve appearance. Stone and pebble mulches, white, gray, or rose-pink, are ornamental.

The only disadvantage of a mulch is that you cannot readily see or feel soil to check for dryness. To determine this, brush a little of the mulch aside. A pot set in a large container and then mulched retains soil moisture longer. Though a practical device anywhere, mulches are essential in hot, dry climates.

Plants in containers require daily attention. Since they are on display, they must always look their best. Water regularly. Without enough moisture, in one scorching weekend lantanas and fuchsias in hanging baskets will wither, turning brown later; wilted petunias and browallias are unlikely to revive when watered again.

[OPPOSITE] *Container gardening is easier if you have an outdoor potting area where soil ingredients and supplies are handy.*

It's a good idea to keep two or more filled watering cans at hand, selecting decorative ones that can be considered garden accessories.

HOW TO WATER

YOU CAN water with a soaker attached to the end of a hose. To avoid stooping get the long-handled kind; these do the job quickly. Removing the nozzle from the hose works well with large plants; where mulches are used, soil spattering is avoided.

The fine spray of a sprinkler is practical if you let it run in one spot for at least half an hour, but use it only where it will not stain

Potted geraniums plunged in the ground fill bare spots left by spring bulbs. Peat moss mulch keeps the soil moist longer so that watering is not so urgent in dry weather.

A decorative stone mulch around a large fuchsia plant holds moisture in the soil and checks weed growth.

or rip large flowers, such as hybrid petunias. Sprinkling removes dust during dry periods, and its overall effect is refreshing to plants. Small pots can be immersed to the brim in a pail, basin, or trough until the soil is well soaked; this is indicated when air bubbles cease to appear. Use this treatment for plants that have dried to the wilting point. But avoid overwatering, as it causes rotting of roots and poor growth. If containers have adequate layers of drainage, water seeps through safely and quickly.

The amount of water needed varies with the size of plant, climate, season, amount of sun, and type of container. Actually, you must water a plant when it needs it, when the soil surface is barely dry; this may be once or twice a day, every other day, or twice a week. In the cool days of spring and autumn and in winter, intervals are longer, especially with evergreens and woody plants in large planters. Where they are needed, place saucers under containers to prevent staining the painted surfaces of porches, tables, and steps. Plastic saucers—dark green, gray, black, or white—are excellent, inexpensive, lightweight, and impervious to water.

FEEDING AND SPRAYING

A WINDOW BOX or other container equipped with a wick and a tray that holds water will keep plants moist longer. The principle is the same as the wick-watering pots for African violets and other house plants. To make a wick-watering window box, two compartments of copper or zinc are needed. The large upper tray that holds the plants and fits into the top of the box has holes at the bottom, about six inches apart, through which nine-inch-long wicks are inserted. These may be of glass wool, the upper end of each wick slit in four places. The bottoms of the wicks rest in the lower four-inch tray that is kept filled with water through the lengthwise slit along the front. To feed plants, about a once-a-month solution of liquid fertilizer, instead of plain water, is poured into the bottom tray. The wicks draw water as needed and keep the plants moist. The plants with root-ball intact are planted preferably in moist vermiculite, which prevents spatter when it rains. With the wick method, plants will last without more water through a long, hot weekend. Generally, trays are filled with water twice a week in summer. The technique avoids drip and is recommended where this is a nuisance.

Feeding pays off. If soil is properly prepared at potting time, plants will probably flourish through one season, but will perform better if fertilized. Since small plants in window boxes, pots, and hanging baskets have restricted root runs, they use up the first supply of nutrients and so benefit from feedings every two or three weeks. Since the life cycle of annuals is short, heavy feeding is not harmful. Trees, shrubs, and large plants, like clivia and agapanthus, also fare better with occasional feeding but not in late summer or fall. Soft, late-season growth is stimulated on woody plants and they are apt to be winter-killed. Whether fertilizer is applied in dry or liquid form, soil must be moist; if it isn't, first water plants thoroughly, allowing them to drain for a few hours before feeding.

If faded blossoms do not drop naturally, as from fuchsias, browallias, and Chinese hibiscus, remove them with fingers, scissors, or pruning shears, and take off any yellow or browning leaves as well. Some plants, like wax begonias, scented geraniums, and coleus, also need regular pinching to encourage branching and maintain symmetrical growth. Notice each plant on your daily watering rounds. Unless checked periodically, many plants quickly grow out of proportion to the size of their containers. Prune back extra long shoots on patience plants and snapdragons, and trim trailers, as vinca, English and Swedish-ivies, and ivy geranium. Prune trees and shrubs to improve their appearance and remove dead and weak wood.

Turn small plants every few days to develop symmetry. Sometimes change locations to give more light or sun or protection from wind. Moving plants around gives you a chance to create a whole new look and this is a fun approach to container gardening.

Plants may need spraying to keep them healthy. If aphids or red spider mites appear, spray with Malathion or Kelthane, or use an all-purpose preparation sold under several trade names. An aerosol bomb containing an all-purpose mixture can be used, but follow directions with care, as spraying too closely may injure foilage or the material may be harmful to certain plants. If you prepare your own spray mixture, you can add a foliar fertilizer to give an extra pickup. Small plants can be immersed in a pail of spray mixture. In general, pests and diseases on container plants outdoors are at a minimum because of the free circulation of air.

With proper care, many plants, as agapanthus, camellia, oleander, and sweet bay, as well as geraniums and lantanas, last for years, even becoming heirlooms in some families. But lack of winter space and the means of regulating temperature are problems. Decide which specimens you care for most, then do the best you can with available facilities.

WINTER AND HOLIDAY CARE

THROUGH the winter, be sure to water hardy outdoor plants in containers—arborvitae, pieris, pines, and yews. Soak the soil well during warm periods and in time of thaws. Plants near buildings, under broad eaves, on porches, and even under laths, dry out more than those set directly in the garden. Rather than depend on nature, keep the watering can and hose handy.

A problem in summer is how to care for containers when you are away for a long weekend, a week, or an extended vacation. Letting plants really dry out sets them back considerably. Some may take weeks to recover; others may die. Try to have some dependable person take over, knowledgeable about plants, if possible, but detailed instructions in writing are a help in any case. In capital letters, direct your helper not to rely on rain, unless it is exceptionally heavy and lasting.

One possibility is to herd small containers in a car for delivery to a friend. Or temporarily "plant" containers in open ground in partial or complete shade. Pack soil around them and water thoroughly. With a thick mulch, they will keep well for two to three weeks. Or small containers can be placed in bushel baskets or boxes, soaked well and filled in with moist peatmoss or soil. Place in the shade of a tree or building to reduce transpiration. For long weekends, large plants can merely be moved to shade and then soaked, since soil for trees and shrubs in large planters remains moist longer than that of small plants.

Another method is to soak soil and wrap pots with bags or sheets of plastic, securing it around the base of plants with string or wire. Then group plants in the shade of a tree or on the north side of a house; there they will stay fresh for a week. Covering tops with plastic cuts down transpiration. With plastic, just be certain plants are in complete shade, as plastic overheats in sun and causes burning. Yet another aid is to cut back the tops of plants to give roots less foliage to maintain. Hanging baskets need special attention. Set them on the ground in a sheltered, shady location and water thoroughly before you go away for a few days. For longer periods engage a plant sitter.

PLANTS FOR OUTDOOR CONTAINERS

(Check your area for information on local hardiness; * indicates tenderness.)

TREES

Acacia*
Arborvitae
Australian pine*
Avocado*
Chamaecyparis
Cherry
Citrus*
Crabapple
Cryptomeria
Dogwood
Ficus*
Fig*
Frangipani*

Ginkgo
Hawthorn
Hemlock
Holly
Italian cypress*
Jacaranda*
Japanese plum*
Linden
Magnolia
Maple
Mountain-ash
Moraine-locust
Norfolk-Island pine*

Oak
Olive
Palm
Pine
Pomegranate*
Redbud
Russian-olive
Silverbell
Sourwood
Spruce
Strawberry-tree*
Styrax
Willow

SHRUBS

Amelanchier
Azalea
Barberry
Bayberry
Boxwood
Camellia*
Chinese hibiscus*
Clethra
Croton*
Crape-myrtle*
Cytisus
Daphne

Deutzia
Elaeagnus
Euonymus
Flowering quince
Franklinia
Fringe-tree
Gardenia*
Hydrangea
Hypericum
Ixora*
Juniper
Leucothoe

Lilac
Mock-orange
Mountain-laurel
Nandina*
Oleander*
Osmanthus*
Pieris
Pittosporum*
Privet
Pyracantha
Rhododendron
Roses

SHRUBS (*continued*)

Skimmia*
Swedish-myrtle

Tibouchina*
Viburnum

Witch-hazel
Yew

VINES

Actinidia
Akebia
Allamanda*
Bignonia*
Bittersweet
Bougainvillea*
Boston ivy
Cardinal-climber*
Chinese fleece-vine
Clematis

Climbing hydrangea
Climbing rose
Cobaea*
Cypress-vine*
English ivy
Euonymus
Gloriosa*
Grape
Honeysuckle
Jasmine*

Moonflower*
Morning-glory*
Nasturtium*
Passion-vine*
Potato-vine*
Stephanotis*
Sweet pea
Trumpet-vine
Wisteria
Woodbine

FLOWERING PLANTS

Achimenes
Agapanthus
Ageratum
Anthurium
Begonia
Bird-of-paradise
Browallia
Brunfelsia
Calceolaria
Calla-lily
Canterbury-bells
Chrysanthemum
Cineraria
Cleome
Clivia
Cosmos
Dahlia
Daylily
Dutch bulbs
Echeveria

Epiphyllum
Episcia
Eucharis
Fall aster
Flowering maple
Flowering tobacco
Forget-me-not
Gazania
Geranium
Gerbera
Ginger
Gladiolus
Heliotrope
Iresine
Iris
Ismene
Kalanchoe
Lantana
Liatris

Lily
Lobelia
Marguerite
Marigold
Montbretia
Nemesia
Patience plant
Phlox
Primrose
Salvia
Showy stonecrop
Shrimp-plant
Snapdragon
Stock
Sweet alyssum
Thunbergia
Tuberose
Tuberous begonia
Zinnia

FOLIAGE PLANTS

Alocasia	German ivy	Salad burnet
Alternanthera	Grape ivy	Santolina
Aluminum plant	Gynura	Schefflera
Artemisia	Hosta	Sempervivum
Aspidistra	Iresine	Setcreasea
Begonias	Jade plant	Spathiphyllum
Bromeliads	Kangaroo-ivy	Sprenger asparagus
Caladium	Lemon verbena	Strawberry
Calathea	Nephytis	Strawberry begonia
Castor-bean plant	Parsley	Summer cypress
Coleus	Philodendron	Sweet bay
Costmary	Pick-a-back	Swedish-ivy
Dumb cane	Podocarpus	Ti-plant
Dusty miller	Pothos	Tradescantia
Fern	Rosemary	Vinca
Fuchsia	Sage	

FOR HANGING BASKETS

Flowering plants for sun

Annual phlox
Bougainvillea
Cascade chrysanthemum
Dimorphotheca
Ivy geranium
Lantana
Lobelia
Monkey flower
Nasturtium
Oxalis
Pansy
Petunia
Pink
Shrimp-plant
Sweet alyssum
Tomato 'Tiny Tim' (fruit)
Verbena

Foliage plants for sun

Donkeytail (*Sedum morganianum*)
English ivy
Flowering inch plant (*Tradescantia blossfeldiana*)
Peppermint geranium
Purple passion-plant (*Gynura sarmentosa*)
Purpleheart (*Setcreasea purpurea*)
Siebold sedum
Sprenger asparagus
Vinca

Flowering plants for shade

Achimenes
Black-eyed Susan vine (*Thunbergia*)
Browallia
Columnea
Episcia
Flowering maple
Fuchsia
Patience plant
Star-of-Bethlehem (*Campanula isophylla*)
Torenia
Tuberous begonia

Foliage plants for shade

Boston fern
Christmas cactus
English ivy
Epiphyllum
German ivy
Golden archangel (*Lamium galeobdolon variegatum*)
Grape ivy
Inch plant
Kangaroo-ivy
Pick-a-back
Pothos
Rabbit's-foot fern
Rosary vine
Spider plant (*Chlorophytum*)
Swedish-ivy
Strawberry begonia
Zebrina

INDEX

ABOUT THE AUTHOR

GEORGE TALOUMIS of Salem, Massachusetts, is a free-lance garden and travel writer, lecturer, and, above all, an expert photographer. He received a B. A. degree from Tufts University, an M. A. from Harvard University, and studied horticulture at the University of Massachusetts.

A former editor of *Horticulture* magazine and publicity director for the Spring Flower Show of the Massachusetts Horticultural Society, he is now garden columnist for the Boston *Globe*. He contributes frequently to garden publications—*Flower and Garden, Grounds Maintenance, Home Garden, Horticulture,* and to the garden sections of *The New York Times* and the *Los Angeles Times*. His feature articles have also appeared in *Down East* and *Yankee*. His first book on container gardening, *Outdoor Gardening in Pots and Boxes,* was published in 1962.

The author has traveled widely in this country and abroad, both in Europe and the Orient, and wherever he goes he studies and photographs plants and gardens. Recently, he led a garden tour to Japan and Hawaii. The many handsome illustrations in this book are evidence of his many interests and great skill with his camera.